Rapid
RESPONSE

Also by Simon Rae

Poetry

Soft Targets (illustrated by Willie Rushton) 1991

Anthologies (Editor)

The Orange Dove of Fiji
(Poems for the Worldwide Fund for Nature) (1989)

The Faber Book of Drink, Drinkers and Drinking (1991)

The Faber Book of Murder (1994)

The Faber Book of Christmas (1996)

General

Dorset of One Hundred Years Ago (1993)

Rapid RESPONSE

Poems from the Guardian 1991-1996

by **Simon Rae**

HEADLAND

First published in 1997
by
HEADLAND PUBLICATIONS
38 York Avenue, West Kirby,
Wirral, Merseyside, L48 3JF

British Library Cataloguing in Publication Data
A full CIP record for this book is available
from the British Library

ISBN 0 903074 96 6

HEADLAND acknowledges the financial
assistance of North West Arts Board

Distributed in the U.K. by Password (Books) Ltd
23 New Mount St., Manchester M4 4DE

Designed and Typeset by Richard Lloyd-Jones

Printed in Great Britain by
L. Cocker & Co., Berry Street, Liverpool

Contents

INTRODUCTION

My first poem appeared in the *Guardian* in 1988 and I have contributed poems to the paper on a regular basis since the December of that year, when Alan Rusbridger launched the Saturday supplement. A selection, with cartoons by Willie Rushton, was published under the title *Soft Targets* at the end of 1991. A second selection seemed overdue. This is it.

All but two of these poems appeared in the Weekend section of the *Saturday Guardian.* I put it like that because at some stage during the period they cover (1991-1996) the Saturday tabloid changed its name from *Weekend Guardian* to *Guardian Weekend.* There have been other changes. With the introduction of colour printing my deadline lengthened from three days to eight. The poem slot was also moved, from near the front of the magazine to the Last Word section at the back. My contributions were reduced from once a week to once a fortnight, and finally to once a month. I now fall into a rota with John Hegley, Anne MacManus and A.N.Other. All of these changes have had the welcome effect of reducing the pressure on me, but they have had knock-on effects on the poems as well. It is obviously less easy to be topical eight days ahead of publication, and less important too, in a slot given over to a more quirkily personal perspective on the world. Over the last two years I have drawn much more on my own experience rather than hammering away at public issues.

This has been no bad thing. Sniping at a corrupt and corrupting government week after week can get wearisome, however willingly it supplies the targets - whether it be selling arms to Iraq and then lying about it; or selling council houses for votes, then lying about it; or selling the privilege of asking questions in the House of Commons then lying about it; or cutting the pensions of war veterans, then lying about it. In all these and other instances, the broadsheet section of the paper has led the way in exposing and condemning the guilty parties (or rather, party). There's not much a poem can add to a front page headline denouncing an MP as 'A Liar and a Cheat'. Indeed, a poet would need the pen of Pope and the scope of *The Dunciad* to do justice to the abject shambles of Conservative rule.

While not operating with that sort of weaponry, I have, I hope, voiced some of the anger and frustration people have felt at the shameful way the Conservative ideology of pure selfishness has undermined our society, with its lottery mentality of It Could Be You replacing traditional concepts of a social contract. For all its window-dressing the Conservative philosophy has been very simple - a creed of ruthless self-interest which has marginalised the weakest and poorest, elevated the already wealthy, and seen a full-scale onslaught on hospitals, schools, prisons, public servicing broadcasting, traditional industries, transport, and the general social fabric alike. It has been an unedifying period, during which Britain has become, without question, a nastier place to live.

I am well aware that I have not covered, let alone covered adequately, half the crying scandals of the squalid mess. This cannot pretend to be the definitive response to the malaise which is modern Britain. I have by and large chosen what I regard as the best poems, trying to ensure a wide range of topic and form. The poems are reprinted more or less as they first appeared, though I have taken the opportunity to make the odd light revision here and there, and extend the last one, PollUp! Poll Up! as a modest contribution to the run-up to the election. Of the two poems included which did not appear in the *Guardian*, one was commissioned by the *Evening Standard*, another by BBC 1's *Breakfast News*. Both were written in my *Guardian* style, and either could have appeared in the paper.

A new departure for me was Sue Casson's development of a musical stage show based on my Weekend poems. Produced by Tom Blackmore, this was performed by a gifted and committed cast on the Edinburgh Fringe and then in London in the second part of 1996. My thanks to all involved.

I would also like to thank Kathy Davies, for coming up with the title; Janice Thomson for being there when it counted and for writing most of the Humphrey poem; my mother Jill Rae, still keeping the scrapbook; and the ever-loyal Harish Shah, as faithful a fan as any writer could possibly wish for; Gladys Mary Coles for having the faith to publish the book.

My thanks also go to Deborah Orr, the current editor of the *Guardian Weekend*, for sticking with me (and for sticking up for me in the face of occasional reader hostility), to Billy Mann, the editor of the Last Word section, and to all those who have had to wrestle poetry's angularities into the straitjacket of newspaper columns. Stuart Legge had this unenviable task in my early days, and he was a pleasure to work with, and a delight to meet when we finally did. His sudden death was very sad and a great shock.

Another terrible shock was the death of Willie Rushton. The book was being prepared for the press at the time, and Willie was looking forward to doing the cartoons for it when he died. He was an extraordinary man, and extremely generous with his many talents. I was lucky enough to do two short runs with him at Edinburgh, and appearing on stage with him was an undiluted joy. I have decided, rather than try to find another cartoonist to step into the breach, to leave the poems without illustration as an eloquent testimony to his incomparable brilliance.

Some of the poems have been reprinted in various anthologies and magazines, and my thanks go to those editors who had the courtesy to ask my permission and found the time to send me copies of their publications when they appeared.

THE DIVERTING HISTORY OF JOHN MAJOR
(With apologies to William Cowper)

*John Major's premiership started with the Tory party
racked with strife over Europe, and looks as though it
will end the same way. His main problem at the outset
was his predecessor, Mrs Thatcher.*

John Major is a citizen
Of credit and renown.
The Tory leader eke is he
In famous London Town.

His wife estranged called Margaret
Had been besotted once,
But now regards this pleasant man
As something of a dunce.

"John, John," she oft reproaches him,
"You're far too easily led;
You'd never stray with foreigners
When we were safely wed."

He soon replies: "I have admired
Of womankind but one,
And you are she, my dearest dear,
But that is all now done.

For since you left the old address
And gave the keys to me
You've said the most appalling things
About me on tv.

I have a journey now to make
To Bonn and eke to Rome."
"Federalist!" she hissed at him,
"Your place is here at home."

John Major gave his horse a kick,
The beast it gave a neigh,
Then half the neighbours standing by
Cried, "Ride the other way!"

But as the mount turned round once more,
Quaint Margaret was seen
Displaying a bloodstained Union Jack
And portrait of the Queen.

The beast reared up in horror then
And off John Major flew.
"Maastricht or Margaret," someone said,
"Will be the death of you."

[30 November 1991]

DELETE 'WILD BELLS'

(With apologies to Alfred Lord Tennyson)

Batting for Britain at Maastricht with Douglas Hurd, Major offered the deadest of dead bats, opting out of anything - most notably the Social Chapter - that offended his Conservative sensibilities.

Ring out, wild bells, to the wild sky.
Delete "wild bells" - extravagant.
Tell them, Douglas, what we want:
Restraint, small print, a tone that's dry.

Ring out the old, ring in the new.
Steady, steady, not so fast,
We rather like the dusty past.
Let's grant the status quo its due.

Ring out the grief that saps the mind,
For those that here we see no more.
We'll drink to that, please lock the door,
To keep out those we left behind.

Ring out the feud of rich and poor,
Ring in redress for all mankind.
We can't sign that commitment blind,
It smacks too much of Jaques Delors.

Ring out the slowly dying cause,
And ancient forms of party strife.
We will sign that bit; strife is rife
When Mrs Thatcher bares her claws.

Ring in sweet manners, purer laws.
We've always done things our own way -
Long hours, inequitable pay.
We want an opt-out from that clause.

Ring out the want, the care, the sin,
  The faithless coldness of the times.
We still have stakes in foreign climes;
We don't want you lot butting in.

Ring in the valiant man and free,
  The larger heart, the kindlier hand.
How good of them to understand.
You know I think they must mean me!

[14 December 1991]

NATIVITY PLAY

With the exception of the all-too-brief cease-fire, the Major years have been marred by continuing violence generated by the conflict in Northern Ireland. A particularly horrific incident occurred over the Christmas period in 1991.

'Boy of 8 shot by Belfast pub gunman' - headline

The way is all so very plain
That we may lose the way.
   G.K.Chesterton, 'The Wise Men'

Step softy through the dreary night,
   To find the place where men can kill;
Gathered in the friendly light,
   Victims you can shoot at will.

Oh, we have learnt to peer and pore
   On prejudices from our youth,
Despising all known forms of Law.
We are the dreary men of gore,
   Maiming, murdering for Truth.

A snooker table at an inn,
   Child or man, it matters not;
Some say vengeance is a sin,
   But we say it is not.

Adherence to a simple code
   Of mayhem and destruction sees us
Once again upon the road,
Like the wise men with their load
   Of presents for the Infant Jesus.

[28 December 1991]

A DOCTOR WRITES

*New Year always brings its crop of articles on how to
survive "the festivities." A particularly unhelpful piece,
by a London GP, appeared this year, peddling such
wide-of-the-mark warnings as "Energetic dancing can
fracture your shinbones; champagne corks can injure
your eyes." Why stop there? I thought.*

Dancing can fracture your shinbones,
Champagne corks can put out your eyes;
And any poor sap who thinks different
Is in for a nasty surprise.

It's been shown if you take a large hammer
And hammer a nail through your toe,
Whatever the aim of your journey,
The pace of your trip will be slow.

And stubbing your old cigarettes out
On a knee or a thigh or a palm,
Will confirm what all doctors will tell you:
It's a habit that causes much harm.

Alcohol too has its dangers -
My readers will hardly need proof -
And medical experts all reckon
You'd better keep drunks off the roof.

While those who by folly are tempted
To marinate slowly in Scotch
Are at risk of spontaneous combustion.
That is the sympton to watch.

Avoid putting hands in the toaster,
The thing is meant only for bread;
And don't wash your hair in neat brandy
And then put a match to your head.

My advice as a GP is simple:
Be careful, whatever you do.
Turn your back on the dangers I've outlined
And you might - just - survive '92.

[4 January 1992]

THE ALTERNATIVE VERSION

A leading literary magazine used Philip Larkin's most famous line in a subscription campaign. The Advertising Standards Authority found, rather late in the day, that this was unacceptable. With the help of Alan Jenkins, I wrote them a less offensive version.

They tuck you up, your mum and dad.
  They always meant to and they do.
Hot-water bottles that they had
  They thoughtfully slip in with you.

And they were tucked up in their turn
  And coddled when they had sore throats,
By parents who, though sometimes stern,
  Made sure they always wore their coats.

Man hands on teddy-bears to man.
  They nod along the nursery shelf.
Get going as early as you can,
  And have a lot of kids yourself.

[25 January 1992]

THIS SPORTING LIFE

*In April 1992 the General Election campaign coincided with
the Grand National. I hedged my bets.*

Major's grey mare, Wobbly Soapbox,
Looks as though it's had a fright.
Coming on the inside bravely,
Kinnock's Rose is dynamite.

Paddy Ashdown's riding surely,
Urging Trojan Horse to move.
Patten on The Party Chairman
Has an awful lot to prove.

John Smith's Budget scrapes the fences;
Promises like divots fly.
Don't investigate too closely
Or you'll get one in the eye.

That's the only Budget showing:
Chancellor Lamont's mount tossed
Its jockey off into the punters
As the Melling Road was crossed.

Kenneth Baker's trailing badly;
He might like to change his spots.
The next five years may well be painful,
Watching others call the shots.

Heseltine's Blond Bomber's snorting,
Fetlock deep in foam and gore.
Win or lose this current battle,
He may win a later war.

So the leaders charge for glory,
Argy-bargy at The Chair.
This, alas, is not the fable
Of the tortoise and the hare.

Far behind trail rank outsiders,
Green Agenda, Global Bane, -
All lost sight of in the melee:
The money's gone on Short Term Gain.

[4 April 1992]

IN MEMORIAM

Francis Bacon, possibly Mrs Thatcher's least favourite modern painter, died on Tuesday, 28 April.

"The man who paints those dreadful pictures"
Finally has gone to rest,
Heeding not La Thatcher's strictures.
He is numbered with the blessed

- Or at least, amid Time's carnage,
Numbered with the few who'll last
When the kindergarten garbage
Down the long black chute is cast.

Thousands queued for retrospectives,
Hungry for an art that shocks
And captures better some perspectives
Than those melting Dali clocks.

From across the room a portrait,
Face besmirched and body slewed,
Beacons out above the fourth-rate,
Talentless and wholly pseud.

Brilliantly the vivisector's
Cold-room imagery appals.
Does it whisper to collectors
"Memento mori" from their walls?

Drinking chums he loved more dearly
Than the rich who paved his way,
Those for whom fine art is merely
Pay, and when you've paid, display.

Screaming popes and meat on platters,
Bare rooms set aside for pain:
In the life, which also matters,
Gambling, Soho and champagne...

[2 May 1992]

21

POME: THE MERSEY MUSE

To mark the 25th anniversary of the THE MERSEY SOUND by Adrian Henri, Roger McGough and Brian Patten.

The Muse was a librarian
Stuck inside dusting books;
She didn't like her job
And she didn't like her looks.

Three likely lads
Just happened by.
They peered through the window
Said My,my,my...

Hey up there, girl,
The party's begun;
Come out and join us
And have some fun.

Forget all the oldies
Writing meaningful reams
- About as exciting
As second-hand dreams.

She put Donald Davie
Back on the shelf;
Said it's time for a girl
To look after herself.

She took off her specs
And drank gin in the bath
And the pomes she wrote,
They made people laugh.

She made love on the ferry
And love on the bus
And when people stared
Said What's all the fuss?

She could rhyme
She could scan,
But if she didn't feel like it she'd just do her nails
and say "I'm not bothered. Girrus a kiss!"

And sometimes she'd
joinupallthewordsinthelinelikethis.

Now she's been swinging
For 25 years,
So to Roger, and Brian
and Adrian: Cheers!

[16 May 1992]

BANGKOK NIGHTS

*May saw another Third World democracy movement
crushed on the streets. As usual we watched it on tv in
perfect safety.*

A frivolous, suggestive name,
Synonymous with what you please
In tacky tourist sex: Bangkok,
The Third World capital of sleaze.

The documentaries show the girls
Sitting, bored, in languid rows,
And beefy, red-necked Western men
Queuing up to see the shows.

But now the story-line has changed;
Quite different images appear:
Defiant crowds at barricades,
Their outrage cancelling their fear.

Such bravery, such sacrifice...
And we look on, appalled, in awe,
As victims of a lawless state
Are murdered in the name of Law.

And which of us, if pushed to it,
Could contemplate that kind of heat -
Confronting real live riot troops
(With real live bullets) on the street?

What's voting worth to you or me?
And would we have the guts to share
The danger and the privilege
Of linking arms across the square?

Absurd, of course. Great battles past
Have long since freed us from our chains.
Democracy is in our blood;
Our blood stays safely in our veins.

And over there? A few fresh graves;
Some limp official protests made;
The streets made safe for Western men
To help the locals with their trade...

[23 May 1992]

OLYMPIC SHAME

Very few people picked up this story which appeared as a filler in The Times. Savvas Saritzoglou, a hammer champion, had the honour of carrying the Olympic flame on the first leg of its journey to Barcelona for the opening ceremony of the 1992 Games. Unfortunately he was caught short after only two miles. A friendly stranger offered to hold the torch for him...

Someone nicked the Olympic flame;
Saw the chance of a moment's fame,
And did the deed and staked his claim.

"I'll hold that." Straight face, no name.
Out of the roadside gents I came,
Only to find he'd taken the flame.

Nothing much happening, life a bit tame,
So he thought he'd knock off the Olympic flame
- Just as I was taking aim.

Excuses are going to sound pretty lame:
Lifted me leg and lost me flame.
The bloke died laughing: what a game!

Someone nicked the Olympic flame.
It's pretty obvious who gets the blame.
Things aren't going to be quite the same

Since someone skedaddled with that flame.
If I ever catch him I vow I'll maim
The thieving bastard who stole my flame

And put me fair and square in the frame,
All my glory curdled to shame
As The Man Who Lost The Olympic Flame.

[13 June 1992]

DAVID GOWER, RECORD BREAKER

After some inexplicable, but hardly untypical, wilfulness
on the part of the selectors, David Gower was recalled
to the Test team. He required 34 runs to overtake
Geoffrey Boycott's record of 8,114 runs for England.

Typical overture, top-edge through slip for four,
King David, forgiven, was back in the swing.
Impassive, inscrutable, quite imperturbable,
Gooch batted on without saying a thing.

Down at the other end, Fortune was Gower's friend -
A snick to the slips was put down on the floor.
He'd given due warning that this was his morning.
The magical target was just thirty-four.

Effortless fluency, justifying truancy
For all of the middle aged schoolboys who gazed
As, eagerly counted up, runs quickly mounted up,
Through consummate stroke-play that left bowlers fazed.

Then came the instant we all wanted desperately -
A shot through the covers imprinted with style.
Boycs' record tumbled then, plodders were humbled when
He lifted his bat with a diffident smile.

[11 July 1992]

LESSONS OF THE WAR
(after Henry Reed)

*"There were 5000 of us and only one toilet." Bosnian
refugee quoted by Maggie O'Kane in the Guardian. As
the Olympics got under way thousands of Bosnians
were being herded into concentration camps.*

Today we have breaking of hearts. Yesterday
We had ethnic cleansing. And tomorrow morning
We shall have what to do after firing the village.
But today we have breaking of hearts. Refugees
Queue at the borders of all of the neighbouring countries,
    And today we have breaking of hearts.

This is the latest agreement, whose purpose
Is beating the clock. Insurgents go rapidly backwards
And forwards assaulting and torching the houses
They call it re-writing the record. And athletes
Go rapidly backwards and forwards, beating the clock
    In order to re-write the records.

This is your sports field today. And this
Is the long-jump pit whose use you will quickly discover
If we hear anyone singing a national anthem
Or wanting the toilet. Anthems are played by the band
(Who've been to the toilet) for every flag on the flagpole,
    Which in our case we have not got.

[1 August 1992]

HISTORY CALLS IN AUGUST
(AGAIN)

"Hello. Remember me? I called last year."
Same combat boots, same torn and bloodied shirt.
O God, I thought, it's History again.
He took my hand and squeezed. It hurt.

"So, how d'you think it's going?" He grabbed a chair.
I offered him some tea. "Last year was tame
In retrospect. That Russian coup looked great,
But then it petered out - a shame.

But this year, Pow! Somalia, the Serbs -
Don't you love the Serbs? - and still Hussein
It's brilliant! Take a gander at the map:
The war zone's spreading like a stain.

The New World Order - What a song and dance!
D'you really think this sort of thing will end?
Mortars into ploughshares. Is it likely?
Pull the other one my friend.

The Cold War's over. Whoopee, Peace! you thought.
You mutts. You think that I would be denied?
As long as there are guns to fire, I'll shoot.
Testosterone personified,

That's me - two sugars, ta, - I like to feel
The rocket fuel of violence in my veins.
I love it all, the screams, the flames, the bangs,
The fresh blood running down the drains,

The queues of refugees, the floating corpses.
Do I repeat myself? Then I repeat
Myself. The point I'm making is: I like
A kitchen where you feel the heat."

He looked round mine and drained his mug of tea.
"Off back to work." He raised a dirty paw.
"Watch out for Sarajevo now!" He winked,
Then turned. He didn't shut the door.

[22 August 1992]

29

EPITHALAMIUM
For Michael and Sara Adams

*Two friends fortuitously elected to get married on my
fortieth birthday, thus providing me with a party I didn't
have to organise. As the day happened to fall on a
Saturday, a poem seemed appropriate.*

I occupy a smoke-filled bar
Whose average age I've just increased,
Reflecting as I stub my fags,
I'm half way through the life I've leased.

Time for change. But time is change,
Implacable as any weather.
Some face the music on their own;
Others choose to march together.

The generations grow like grass.
We all confront time's lawnmower.
Some seed takes hold on fertile ground;
Some falls on stony. Blame the sower.

Whatever makes the garden grow,
Whatever fuels the loving-cup,
There are no short-cuts on the road
(And both should do the washing up).

Cynics doubt all such commitments;
Love is only for the birds.
I can't refute that, but I offer
What I can: the gift of words.

Trellised round an ancient frame,
A benediction in a stanza.
From this shared day may your lives prove
A conjugal extravaganza.

[12 September 1992]

BALLAD OF REDUNDANCY

"4,600 job losses announced" - typical headline.
And the recession ground on.

The day of the redundancy
  The sky grew dark. It rained.
Sales figures, graphs and pie charts:
  You didn't need it explained.

Draw a line through next month's diary,
  Pull the calendar down from the wall;
Cast around for someone to blame,
  But it's nobody's fault at all.

Clear the desk of pens and photos -
  The smiling kids, the wife.
Pack them away in the briefcase:
  They're yours for the rest of your life.

Twenty odd years of service,
  And you're left with idle hands.
A career in the end comes down to a pile
  Of paper-clips, rubber-bands.

Eyes go shy in the office;
  It's a shame no one wants to share.
Keep it all bottled up inside,
  Though you'd like to sling a chair

- One of those heavy revolving ones -
  Right through that window pane,
On the other side of which
  Continues to fall the rain.

[10 October 1992]

TARZAN REFLECTS

The Tory Party Conference this year had an understandably triumphalist ring, but there were clearly perils ahead for the newly re-elected Prime Minister, not least from his closest rival in the leadership contest, Michael Heseltine. Jokingly playing down any potential rivalry, he urged Heseltine: "Come on Michael! Out with your club, on with your loin-cloth! Swing into action!"

All right, I'll get my loin-cloth on,
And I'll unsheath my fearsome chopper.
You'll glimpse it flashing through the trees.
It really is a handsome whopper.

I'll swing with one arm waving by
And clear the jungle of red tape.
Oh sure; but I'll do more than that
To lick the country into shape.

"President" I like - a lot;
But Board of Trade? I'm bored of trade.
I crushed the miners underfoot, ·
A triumph that will never fade;

I saw the blue-rinse tigress off;
I was the Man called by the Hour,
I was the one who did the deed.
I have an appetite for power.

The back-bench monkeys chatter madly,
The cry goes up: Drift at the top!
A valid point. That dozy sloth
Lamont looks ready for the chop.

Clarke the baboon may beat his chest
And show his brightly coloured bum,
But seriously rival me?
That hairy ape? Come come, come come.

Higher still, a head pokes through
Belonging to a proud giraffe.
Well, Douglas certainly has style.
But match for me? Don't make me laugh.

And that leaves only one remaining
Of all this unimpressive zoo.
Me Tarzan, sure, Prime Minister,
But what, I ask, does that make you?

[24 October 1992]

EMBARGOES

(after John Masefield)

The Arms-to-Iraq scandal rumbled on throughout this Parliament, throwing up increasingly embarrassing evidence, but never quite delivering the ministerial resignations that might have been expected.

Dodgy British shipments breaking the embargo,
Sneaking by the backdoor into old Baghdad,
With a cargo of helmets,
Machine tools, spare parts -
Every last requirement can be had.

Confidential papers coming from the court case,
Tipping off the public that a minister can lie,
With a smoke-screen of half-truths,
Own-goals, cover-ups
From Heseltine, Ridley and the DTI.

Dirty British scandal with a red-faced front bench,
Huffing through the Commons in their brusque bluff way,
With bucketfuls of whitewash,
Promising inquiries,
Putting off till next year Judgment Day.

[21 November 1992]

HANDING OVER *(Bush to Clinton)*
Message found on the Oval Office desk

I left things ticking over
(The way a time-bomb ticks).
But that's the only way to learn
The big world's dirty tricks.

Yes, things are going quite nicely.
I left them on the boil,
To show you our inheritance
Means desert sands and oil.

Things look very different
From the deck of Air Force One.
Being President has got some perks,
And running wars is one.

The problems, though, are legion:
Recession, healthcare, AIDS...
It's more than just adoring crowds
And flashy motorcades.

(Sure you risk being shot at,
But mostly gunmen fail.
You're pretty safe when next to you
Is standing J. Dan Quayle.)

Other pressing worries -
A matter for regret,
Ronnie's little over-spend,
The record National Debt.

It's not a bed or roses.
The buck, of course, stops there -
Just where you are sitting now,
Right there, in my old chair.

So long, you've got a plateful;
Good luck, you can but try.
I'm leaving you my number, Son.
I'm always there. Goodbye.

[30 January 1993]

FAILING THE TEST

*Controversy surrounded the omission of David Gower
from the winter tour of India. England lost the first Test
in Calcutta by 8 wickets. It was Graham Gooch's 100th
Test match, but not one he is likely to want to remember,
even though he was presented with a copy of
Rabindrinath Tagore's poems.*

Down by the banks of the Hooghly River
Wanders a man with a face full of woe;
Down by the ghats where the vultures hover,
On he wanders with footsteps slow.

Veteran now of his hundredth Test match,
A hundred Tests, so he knows the score,
He leaves Calcutta with a dented record
And a book of poems by a man called Tagore.

Down by the banks of the Hooghly River
He sees a ghost who shouldn't be there,
A not particularly old ghost either,
Handsome, willowy, debonair.

Hello, old ghost, he calls out softly,
Hello, old ghost, just passing through?
Where were you at Eden Gardens?
Where were you when we needed you?

Where were you when the wickets tumbled?
When the fire-crackers roared and they had us on toast?
Where were you when the crowds exploded?
Where were you when we needed you most?

The ghost just smiled and shrugged his shoulders,
Flicked his wrists as though to say:
Here I am, and here I will be,
Whenever, wherever, you'd like me to play.

[13 February 1993]

0.5 PER CENT

*Against the background of a row over multiple choice
tests in English for fourteen-year-olds, the Government
offered teachers a pay increase of 0.5%*

Is Juliet a Capulet? Is Hamlet a cigar?
And which in your opinion is more utterly bizarre,
This way of testing kids on what great Shakespeare might
have meant,
Or denigrating teachers with just 0.5 per cent?

On Friday afternoons when clocks go slow or simply stop,
It's difficult to concentrate on leagues and coming top.
But no one in the Ministry seems likely to relent,
And furthermore, they're offering just 0.5 per cent.

From Harrogate in Yorkshire down to Tunbridge Wells in Kent,
From Cromer on the Norfolk coast to Pontypool in Gwent,
The teachers, squeezed on every side, are quite right to resent
A snide, insulting pay increase of 0.5 per cent.

[27 February 1993]

THE GOLDEN-AGERS

'If only we could get back to the past, people are saying,
things would be manageable again.'
                                        Martin Kettle, the Guardian.

Back into the golden past
The golden-agers sail,
Returning every time they go
To tell the same old tale -

How twenty, thirty odd years back
No door was ever locked;
How if a scrap of litter fell,
The neighbourhood was shocked;

And criminals (there were a few)
Were highly moral blokes
Who never carried guns or spoiled
The lives of common folks.

But then again, the older ones
Look back before the war
(A peaceful time, the war years were,
When no one ever swore) -

Ah, then society knew respect,
And women knew their place,
And no child ever went to school
Without a polished face.

But greybeards even then droned on
Of life when they were young,
When minors rightly felt the birch
And criminals were hung.

They missed Victoria's golden age
When debtors thronged the Fleet
And little children sold themselves
For pennies on the street.

And skip a century or so,
Nostalgia still looks back
To days when discipline held sway
With branding iron and rack.

[6 March 1993]

PARADISE AUDITED

April Fools' Day marked the dawning of Year Zero at the BBC as John Birt's reforms took effect, and the controversial Producer Choice was introduced. This poem was commissioned by the Evening Standard.

The BBC (that is, Before Birt Came)
Enjoyed a legendary reputation
For squandering cash without the slightest shame
On hospitality and recreation.
It cost a fortune keeping Dylan merry;
The nation's favourite Auntie loved the sherry.

Forget the knees-ups - that was yesterday.
April Fools' Day won't leave things the same.
A new broom enters, set to brush away
Those old excesses of Before Birt Came.
The new regime is strict and pulls no punches.
So no more booze-ups, no more three-hour lunches.

"Integrity and fairness and straight-dealing,
Transparency and openness all round" -
In studios from Maida Vale to Ealing
These are the qualities that will abound,
In studios, of course, that are not closed
As stringent fiscal measures are imposed.

For like the NHS and education
The BBC's become a market place.
With ideology its new foundation,
It's putting on a brave new worldly face.
So competition and efficiency
Are now the buzz words at the BBC.

A man who knows the price of everything
Determines how the future's going to look.
The Corporation's now being made to cling
To one last leaf from Mrs Thatcher's book.
Producer Choice is Birt's Thought for the Day
And Total Costing is the game to play.

The Beeb will invoice everyone in sight
For absolutely anything at all,
Including parking space (you heard me right),
And each square inch of office wall.
While those in charge right-size the structure core
The staff are measuring their office floor.

It's true some sixty million quid last year
Went AWOL, but the paper clips at least
Are now being properly costed, never fear,
And rubber-band efficiency's increased
A hundredfold. A new resource directive
Shows ways to make the Tipp-Ex cost-effective.

Extend this total costing fantasy:
Let's take, for sake of argument, a chair.
A chair costs money, so you charge a fee
To sit on it. Before Birt Came the air
In studios was free. No more. A scale
Of costings (known as Air Time) will prevail

Henceforth. And based upon the average lung
Capacity, they'll monitor each voice
And charge accordingly - presenters, young
And old, will have their rate. Producer Choice
Demands a price for every breath you draw.
They want the bricks; they'll charge you for the straw.

The old regime has gone, and so farewell.
But can you cost an institution's soul?
The men with clipboards ask, What's there to sell?
Refer it back to Quality Control.
Well, we shall know before so very long
If sombre Mr Birt is right or wrong.

[31 March 1993]

LIGHT AT THE END OF THE TUNNEL

'Opening delayed as Eurotunnel blames builders' -
*Guardian headline. Despite another postponement of the
opening of the Chunnel, travel brochures, complete with
details of fares, were promised for the autumn.*

Light at the end of the Chunnel?
The two ends have certainly met,
But as for a date for the opening -
Well, nothing's decided as yet.
Just when they'll be snipping the ribbon
Is frankly anyone's bet.

This triumph of private investment
Has come off the rails once again.
The contractors are claiming more money
For their armies of helmeted men,
While the backers and bankers are yelling
When will you finish, oh when?

The first travel brochures are coming,
Complete with the details of fares,
Which must give some heart to the punters
Who forked out a fortune in shares.
Thousands would love to buy tickets,
But with no bloody trains, no one dares.

In the meantime the factions keep squabbling -
They've got all their lines learnt by rote;
And the companies running the ferries
Have given up trying not to gloat.
Their message is perfectly simple:
If you want to see France, go by boat!

[1 May 1993]

44

THE ROLLING ENGLISH ROLLING STOCK
(after G.K.Chesterton)

An all-party select committee condemned the Government's unpopular plans for the privatisation of the railways.

Before the Tories came to power to privatise BR
The network was extensive and its services stretched far.
You might not make it there on time, you might not travel fast,
But British Rail heroically would get you there at last:
A mazey trip, a lazy trip, from Cumbria to Kent,
A journey you could make by way of Hull or Stoke-on-Trent.

But now the Government intends to privatise the lot.
(Do Tory ministers use trains? Quite frankly they do not.)
A dozen different franchises will open up for trade,
And those who buy commuter lines will have their fortunes made.
But woe betide the traveller with foolish thoughts to wend
By dreamy branchlines down the coast from Harlech to Bridgend.

The minister is keen to introduce a new regime
As radical as anything seen since the days of steam:
A ruinous, expensive way with ever-higher fares,
And tickets sold in bucket-shops by men with shifty stares.
When the dear old English rolling stock has rattled round the bend
Our public service transport will have reached a bitter end.

[8 May 1993]

NADIR'S GOAT

Asil Nadir, the well-connected businessman
facing fraud charges, left Britain from a private
aerodrome and returned to his native Cyprus,
where he was warmly feted and presented with a
goat to sacrifice. He generously reprieved the
beast, and when the Lord Chancellor, who was
also on the island attempted to persuade him to
return, offered the goat instead.

Picture me grazing the back yard
And moodily straining my tether,
Fretful, scuffing my shadow,
Bored of the flies and the weather,

When all of a sudden, commotion
Ruptured the afternoon heat,
And a group waving placards and shouting
Were on me before I could bleat.

You could see they were all pretty merry
And having a bit of a gloat.
Round here having a party
Means only one thing - a goat.

They took me down to the villa.
You don't get much choice when you're trussed.
I bucked a bit for the cameras,
But they threw down in the dust.

By nature I'm not optimistic;
As a scapegoat I do know the score.
No one needed to tell me
Exactly what they had in store.

It was then that the miracle happened.
Just as they stretched out my throat,
The man from Del Monte restrained them:
"We don't want to kill that nice goat."

As they were untying the halter
A dour-looking stranger passed by.
"I have come for that bail-jumping miscreant,
And my name," said the man, "is Mackay."

He was wearing what some folk mistook for
My kid-brother's rear on his head.
"But I'm staying here," laughed Mr Nadir.
"Here's the goat; take him back instead."

[22 May 1993]

MEMOIRS ARE MADE OF THIS

Mrs Thatcher brought out the first volume of her Memoirs to coincide with the autumn conference season.

You thought that she'd gone, that she really retired?
Oh no, Mrs Thatcher's refuelled and rewired.
"Don't worry," she says, with those steely blue eyes,
"Granny will always be here to advise."

The advance was enormous and so was the hype,
And it gave Mrs Thatcher the freedom to snipe:
The folly of Lawson, the malice of Howe,
And then, how appallingly things are done now.

The drifting of Major, the weakness of Hurd;
The idea of anyone else is absurd.
Turn page after page, it's a blast from the past,
Which may well leave some open-mouthed and aghast.

It's Mrs T's veiled manifesto, of course,
A handbag in hardback delivered with force.
How desperately Granny would like to come back
To restore former glories with hair-pull and smack.

[23 October 1993]

THE MORAL MAZE

Justice Minister David MacLean made the astonishing claim that politicians had stepped in to fill the moral vacuum left by the church.

The Church has long since lost its way
With sociology
Replacing as its stock in trade
Old-style theology.

What's more they don't believe in God,
But Tory MPs do.
God's in his heaven and the sky
Is mercifully blue.

Our politicians, pure as snow,
All know the price of sin.
At least they know the cost of it
When trying to get back in.

The trendy Church sits on the fence,
And softly clears its throat.
But MPs talk of "black and white"—
It's often worth a vote.

Yes, their theology is sound,
They know it all too well:
Heaven's a majority
And oppostion Hell.

Sack the bishops, every one;
They're out of step this time.
The pulpits should be manned by men
Who won't be soft on crime.

These paragons of probity
Will lead the moral fight -
The only ones in these dark days
Who'll tell you wrong from right.

[4 December 1993]

THE UMPTEEN DAYS OF CHRISTMAS

Rejoice, rejoice! Great news we bring, the Herald Angels said,
But clearly they were not empowered to look this far ahead
To Jingle Bells in shopping malls, the Yuletide shopping spree,
The moulded plastic reindeers and the tinsel Christmas tree.

One straw-filled manger, fair enough; one Saviour Child, OK,
But why this ghastly rigmarole en route for Christmas Day?
The whisky-breathing Santas on their grotty grotto's throne
Dispensing Christmas greetings in a grotty glottal drone;

The cards piled up in tottering towers on every kitchen table
Depicting snowbound shepherds grouped like gnomes
                                          around the stable,
And lists of presents that resemble blackmailers' demands
Drawn up according to the television ads' commands;

The climb into the loft to search for last year's paper chains
And fairy lights you barely trust to plug into the mains,
And turkeys like prop-forwards hung in every butcher's shop,
And everybody running round and wishing it would stop.

Yes, Christmas, if it really came but one day in the year
Might actually be the cause of genuine good cheer.

[11 December 1993]

CHRISTMAS CARDS

I'm looking at a pile of Christmas cards.
So what? That's not so strange a thing to do.
The trouble is, these Christmas cards go back
To - who'd believe it? - 1992.

The ideas was, I'd write to everyone
Who'd kindly sent those Christmas cards to me;
Or if not write then make a lengthy list
Of who'd get cards in 1993.

So what went wrong? They've sat there for a year,
Moved round from table-top to chair to floor
(In-tray of last resort), and I'm afraid
They may be there in 1994.

I'm sorry, I apologise. I'll put
My good intentions into over-drive.
I make this solemn, binding, public pledge:
I will send cards in 1995.

[18 December 1993]

SARAJEVO SUNSET

'Twenty one months of siege, suffering and fear'
The Guardian

The season of good will brought no resolution to the situation in Bosnia, although some civilians were allowed out of Sarajevo as a humanitarian gesture.

The coaches line up nose to tail;
Evacuees have crammed the seats
And wait to take the dangerous trail
In one of hope's forlorn retreats,
To round off yet another year
Of siege and suffering and fear.

"So where were you?" Well, we were here.
The siege was on each TV screen.
We watched the suffering, felt the fear.
You wanted us to intervene?
We simply couldn't. Douglas Hurd
Explained it would have been absurd.

To square the circle of our shame
At standing by with well-rinsed hands,
Our leaders pass the parcel, Blame,
Though no one really understands
Priorities that place prestige
Above your suffering, fear and seige.

So where does that leave us, you ask.
We'll manage some slight offering,
But we're unequal to the task.
We can't allay your suffering.
We fear your fear, and, truth to say,
We wish your seige a world away.

[8 January 1994]

52

CRYING FOUL

There is dog-dirt in the alley
Where you wouldn't want to dally -
A splendid show right opposite my door.
And it drives me quite doo-lally
As I make my little tally
Of the turds, and I can tell you there are four.

And by lunchtime and no later
Some unwary ambulator
Will have met his quietly ponging Waterloo.
Just popped out to buy a paper,
Now he needs a cast-iron scraper
To scrape the unscooped poop from off his shoe.

I would like to ask the owner,
That so anti-social loner,
Just what passes through what passes for his brain,
As his pooch (is it a groaner?)
Does its stuff as pavement-donor:
Does he think the muck will wash off in the rain?

Does he snigger as we tread in it,
Enjoying the casual spread of it;
Does he like to see the pavement dark with smears?
Does he mock our natural dread of it,
Thinking cleanliness instead of it
Would spoil a fine tradition cherished years?

Oh the council takes our taxes
But it utterly relaxes
Any by-laws there may be against this curse.
Should one ring them or send faxes
Or go round with guns and axes?
The situation's bad, and getting worse.

[29 January 1994]

53

A WORD FROM THE BOARDROOM

*At a time of savage 'downsizing', salaries for those at
the very top of the pile rose staggeringly.*

Your life revolves around a simple task
Repeated as by rote hour after hour,
For which you're paid a pittance. Why? you ask.
Because, quite frankly, you are in my power.

And I decide - because that is my role.
I could, if I decided it was best,
Chuck you and all your mates out on the dole
And shut down half the plant and sell the rest.

Decisions are the kind of work I do,
And they determine how our profit's made.
And that is why I have my private loo,
The car, the jet, and why, of course, I'm paid

Enormous sums of money year by year.
My friend, who ever claimed that life was fair?
And if they did, I didn't seem to hear.
It isn't; and what's more I don't much care.

[12 March 1994]

AN ATTORNEY'S SWAN-SONG
(with apologies to Sir John Betjeman)

Sir Nicholas Lyell, the Attorney-General, was the man left facing the embarrassing questions about gagging orders and related matters at the Scott enquiry. He was particularly non-plussed by Scott's assistant, Presily Baxendale.

Sir Nicholas Lyell, Sir Nicholas Lyell,
Attorney renowned for discretion and guile,
A lighthouse, a beacon - or will o' the wisp
When faced with some questioning probing and crisp?

Judge shirty, judge snorty, impatient at least,
At the progress with which the whole truth is released.
He's critical too at gagged papers unread,
And suppression of what it was Heseltine said.

Oh everyone says it's a scandalous case,
But what can the government do to save face?
It's a problem for Major - what is he to do?
- Except find a scapegoat. Now can you guess who?

Sir Nicholas Lyell, Sir Nicholas Lyell,
Tormented by Presily Baxendale's smile,
Her top-spin, her back-hand, her crucifying lob:
Are you really, we wonder, the man for the job?

Oh wouldn't you rather escape from the fray,
Just hand in your racket and saunter away,
To watch others serve as you're sipping your tea,
Relieved to be out of the headlines, Scott-free?

[2 April 1994]

MANDATE

Democracy finally, astonishingly, came to South Africa.

The new day dawns, the big abstractions shine:
Freedom, Justice, Peace, Security...
The Broederbond still hanker for a sign
From the sjambok god of racial purity,
Of dawn raids, bulldozers, whips, dogs and trucks,
Of pass laws, sex laws and the smoking sky
Of violent dispossesion; but their luck's
Leaked out: they've drained their water bottle dry.
The future lives with those long patient queues
Abiding in the sun, hour after hour,
Threading through the planet's nightly news,
Inheriting at last the means to power:
The mystery of a cross against a name.
And nothing now will ever be the same.

[7 May 1994]

LIMERICKS FOR THE CHUNNEL

*The Queen and the French President were finally invited
to open the Channel Tunnel.*

The Queen and the President met.
They paraded, made speeches, and ate.
They got back on the train
And met once again,
Cordiale as two leaders can get.

*

Isambard Kingdom Brunel
Said, "I could have done just as well.
It's only a drain
Designed for a train,
But my blueprint was voted to hell."

*

Count Schlieffen, the military man,
Hoped the thing was a flash in the pan.
"If it ever gets made,
I'd be loath to invade.
The Tunnel would scupper my Plan."

*

The view from the windows might pall.
It undergoes no change at all.
You sit in your seat,
Admiring the feat,
But there's nothing to look at but wall.

[14 May 1994]

IN MEMORIAM: JOHN SMITH

John Smith's death came as a shock to everyone, and he
was mourned across the political spectrum.

Whisky and mountains, family and friends,
Good humour and that warm engaging smile;
No one doubts that politics depends
On personality: we knew your style

Would grow on us. It didn't matter much
When things went quiet and you dropped out of view;
We knew that you were perfectly in touch,
That you were playing it long. We trusted you.

The country in a way kept you on hold.
With you to come they felt they could relax,
And watching poor John Major's fate unfold
Beat any dry debate on health or tax.

The Tory Party's woeful disarray,
Their brilliant deck-chair-in-a-gale routine,
Quite rightly made the running day by day.
But now you've gone, your qualities are seen

For what they were - the best foundation stone
On offer for the future that we had.
You bred a powerful hope where there was none,
And that, for all our grief, should make us glad.

[21 May 1994]

ALAN CLARK HA HA HA

*Alan Clark's sexual peccadilloes detailed in his diaries
caused writs to fly and a great deal of enjoyment to on-
lookers.*

Samuel Pepys employed a code;
Boswell spilled his nightly load
Of guilty resumés of lust
In volumes that then gathered dust

In some ancestral padlocked trunk.
Stone cold sober, reeling drunk,
Philanderers all feel the need
To annotate their carnal greed,

But most prefer to keep the lid
Firmly clamped on what they did
Until they head into the dark.
Not so feisty Alan Clark,

For whom life hasn't been so bad:
A decent fortune from his dad,
(Although he says it's not enough);
A spouse who doesn't cut up rough

About his women on the side,
Apart from making rather snide
Asides about their social class.
And he of course acquired the pass

To open all of Whitehall's doors
And stroll along the corridors
Of power and influence. He made
A bullish Minister of Trade.

Life was really such a breeze.
But now a rising tide of sleaze
Is lapping at the castle walls,
And folk whose attitude appals

Are slinging mud and calling names,
And playing Max Clifford's little games -
Because he opted to expose
Himself to all in candid prose.

Still, whichever side prevails,
The scandal has been good for sales.
The diary's very widely read.
Some cash in hand. And so to bed...

[11 June 1994]

THE LAST POST

*In the craze to sell every last item of the family silver,
the Government had the Post Office in its sights for a
time.*

Beneath the spreading chestnut tree
The village postman props
His bicycle and with his sleeve
His honest brow he mops.

The village down the lane from him
Is drowsing in the heat,
Surrounded by the unhedged fields
Of EC surplus wheat.

Two pensioners are making tracks
Towards the village store
Which doubles as the post office
Where they and others draw

Their weekly pensions and enjoy
The chance to chat awhile.
The village postmistress has time
To serve them with a smile.

A timeless scene you may well think,
Old England at its best.
But once the PO's privatised
It will be laid to rest

Along with other sides of life
Which quietly slipped away
Beneath the cost-efficient axe
Because they didn't pay.

Re-paint the fleets of Royal Mail vans:
It's now called Profit Force.
The village postman and his bike
Will have to go of course.

And let old ladies take the bus
(Though buses now are few)
And bump and bustle into town
To join a proper queue.

[9 July 1994]

WE ALL FALL DOWN

*Reports of a thriving black market in weapons-grade
plutonium from the Soviet Union sent sinister ripples
across the Foreign pages.*

A hotel room, a suitcase, and the haze
Of a dozen untipped chain-smoked cigarettes.
Handshakes, wary smiles - a deal is struck.
They go their separate ways without regrets.

The rest of us drowse on, assured the world's
A safer place to be since the great thaw.
The two antagonists have dropped their guard;
A generation is excused its war.

Another suitcase in another room:
A different group of wild-eyed, hunted men,
Whose tortured vision of true justice brings
The threat of Armageddon round again.

Berlin, London, Paris or New York:
Self-justifying vengeance spins across
The skyline of a great metropolis
The eyeball-melting flash of total loss.

[27 August 1994]

THE IRA CEASEFIRE

But nearer to home, Ireland seemed nearer to peace
with the announcement of the IRA ceasefire.

Will lovers now walk freely down each street
Without the blade of terror at their hearts?
Will total strangers be prepared to meet
Without employing the surreptitious arts
Of mutual scrutiny? Will children's games
Conform more nearly to their mothers' dreams,
And rivalries dissolve into the names
Of fervently supported football teams?
And will the singers find new songs to sing,
And men past work looked forward to slow days
Of wistful, unprovoked remembering?
Will pulpit voices quieten into praise,
And neighbouring church bells ring in harmony?

Those who can will pray so. We shall see.

[10 September 1994]

REMEMBRANCE

*On a trip to San Francisco I visited the home of the
AIDS quilt.*

Last year I walked with friends across
The battlefields of France
And stumbled into trenches which
Held up the planned advance
And stood beneath the edifice
Of cold remembrance,

And in imagination caught
The lonely bugle blown,
Saluting in the evening air
Each name inscribed on stone
Raised above the shovelled flesh
And gathered bone.

Today another battlefield
Where death has taken hold,
Preferring in the usual way
Youth to the earmarked old,
Inflicting through the hapless ranks
A grief untold.

Recruited from 10,000 homes,
This peacetime army heard
The call to one another's arms
Which could not be deferred.
But they too found that death required
The final word.

Their monument is not of stone
Imploring empty sky.
Instead on any public space
The patchwork panels lie
Attesting that these myriad names
Shall never die.

Sewn into vibrant life by love,
The Quilt's their cenotaph.
One grave-sized strip presents a pair
Of jeans and a photograph.
I gazed down at the too-young face
Lit by a laugh.

[5 November 1994]

BACK-BENCH CHORUS

In his Canute-like struggle against the rising tide of sleaze in the Conservative party, the Prime Minister set up the Nolan committee to vet MPs' interests.

We are not ambitious men
(We've no thought of Number 10)
And most of us are back-bench hacks at best.
We like to see our way
To supplement our pay
But now we've got to face this Nolan pest.

We are slaving half the night
In defence of what is right
When we could be city slickers to a man,
And it seems quite fair to me
That we charge a little fee
For being as helpful as - and where - we can.

When we weekend at the Ritz
Or our mistresses have fits
About the kids we never should have had,
And we hog the tabloid pages
Our behaviour quite enrages
Constituents and drives them nearly mad.

But we are human too,
Just like you, or you, or you,
And talk of 'sleaze' can cause us all distress.
Self-regulation's fine,
That's the solid back-bench line.
Far better if Lord Nolan gagged the press.

[28 January 1995]

OVERHEARD IN THE VESTRY

'Anglican bishops re-examine stance on homosexuality'
The Times

O Lord, it seems the pathway up to Thee
Is not as easy as it used to be.
To think our prejudices held so long
Turn out to be, well, if not wholly wrong,
Then not exactly wholly right - or writ.
Dear dear, forgive my feeble shot at wit,
But this new thinking really hasn't hit
The bullseye with our little rural flock.
The headlines gave the Major quite a shock.
He shook the paper underneath my nose
And said, "So, Vicar, any damn thing goes
These days, then, eh?" Thou heardst the whole tirade.
He speaks for quite a few, Lord, I'm afraid.
I've had The Mothers round en masse, as well.
They weren't remotely happy I could tell:
Deep silence, broken by a pointed cough.
I think our first gay wedding's some way off.
I said although Thy ways are sometimes strange
There were some things that wouldn't ever change.
There'll be no hanky-panky with the choir.
And now, Lord, just a word about the spire...

[25 March 1995]

FINGERS

*There were moments when you thought everybody in
the country was at it.*

Fingers in the fleshpots,
Fingers fumbling flies,
Fingers through the pie-crust
Of oh so many pies.

Fingers crossed discreetly,
Fingers greasing palms,
Fingers counting briskly
The loot from selling arms.

Fingers raised in honour,
Fingers raising flags,
Fingers knotting neatly
The throats of bulging bags.

Fingers begging questions,
Fingers licked to count
What by any standards
Is not a small amount.

Fingers fishing fishnets,
Fingers frisking bras,
Fingers in the backseats
Of well upholstered cars.

Fingers in a panic,
Fingers in the air,
Warding off the flashlights'
Sharp intrusive glare...

[20 May 1995]

TELL ME THE TRUTH ABOUT POWER
(With apologies to Auden)

Some say that power's for little boys
    Who never quite grew up.
Some say it's just a background noise,
    While some I asked threw up.
The pollsters trying to decide
    Exactly what is what
Found people on the street replied:
    "Power's what we haven't got!"

Is its manner at parties abrasive?
    Does it loom with a terrifying smile?
Are its answers to questions evasive?
    Are its speeches a horrible trial?
Does it often succumb to distractions?
    Does it think the electorate a shower?
Just what are its greatest attractions?
    Oh tell me the truth about power.

I tried to get the answer straight
    And went to Westminster.
I listened to a long debate:
    The poor Prime Minister
Sat there as though he writhed in flame -
    The things he heard weren't kind.
A (neck-w)ringing endorsement came
    From those who sat behind.

Does it practise its frowns in the mirror?
    Is the word that it uses most "Fair"?
Will it ever admit to an error?
    And is it too proud of its hair?
Does it mean what it says about loyalty?
    Does it match up the Man with the Hour?
Should we give up and leave it to Royalty?
    O tell me the truth about power.

[1 July 1995]

70

COLLEGE GREEN

John Major called a snap election for the leadership of the Conservative party in a vain attempt to restore unity. Camera-hungry Tories had a field day, parading round the clock on College Green. BBC Breakfast News commissioned the following piece.

The camera crews have seen it all before:
One week it's politics, the next it's war.
It's just the media circus's routine:
Last week, Bosnia, this week, College Green.

So this is news. But then, it's also sport.
Forget the plink, plunk, plonk of Centre Court.
I tell you, Wimbledon has never seen
Such battles as the grass of College Green.

The things supporters say may make you wary
(Their dress sense can be positively scary);
Their hair is brushed to a persuasive sheen.
They're groomed vaingloriously for College Green.

Ditherers and "Don't Knows" check their ties
And gallantly rehearse their bare-faced lies -
Nonentities enjoying a chance to preen
Before the Nation's eyes on College Green.

Beyond the clutches of the party whips
Backbenchers smirk and mouth "Just read my lips",
Delighting in the chance to fill the screen
For fifteen seconds down on College Green.

And after all the brouhaha at last
The pleaded-for and promised votes are cast.
The loser contemplates what might have been
As shadows lengthen over College Green.

[5 July 1995]

SHEEP STEALING: THE SILLY SEASON

Damien Hirst kicked up rough over a Boddington's
promotion featuring a sheep in a tank of the Cream of
Manchester.

Art is what the critics say it is.
Art is very serious and posh.
It has to be in order to succeed
In generating large amounts of dosh.

Dead sheep, in case you didn't know, are in,
According to the people who decide.
In what? I hear you ask. Well, in this case,
A fish tank filled up with formaldehyde.

But is it true or beautiful or good?
That's not the point; the point is, it can shock.
Taste's not at issue; no one now will eat
This errant member of the woolly flock.

And recently some very clever ad-man
Decided for a lark that he'd display
A sheep dipped in a tank of Boddingtons.
He thought he'd help to sell the beer that way.

But Baa-Baa Boddington has hit a snag;
According to the arch-installer, Hirst,
You cannot use a submerged sheep to shift
The stock you brewed to quench the nation's thirst.

He has a nerve to copyright all mutton.
I have to say it seems a little steep.
Has anybody canvassed Geoffrey Howe,
Or, come to that, the nation's bleeding sheep?

[15 July 1995]

THE NAKED SHIT POEM

*Gilbert and George put on a show of their Naked Shit
Pictures. I went along to see what all the fuss was about.*

The thing I missed was the smell of it.
Pushed, I suppose I'd have to admit
I found it wasn't the slightest bit

Like shit at all, more browny rocks
Standing as tall as grandfather clocks,
Odd shaped imports down on the docks:

Totem poles, obelisks, ethnic tat.
Difficult grasping that someone shat
Things as straight and as tall as that.

So this is the stuff (we're told) that forges
The New - while tickling bourgeois gorges.
(But which were Gilbert's, which were George's?)

A critic says it's beyond the absurd,
And I suppose we have to take his word.
It takes a critic to pass a turd.

Don't get me wrong, I'm not complaining.
Let's all roll back our potty training
And enjoy the process as we're straining -

Cherish each plop and savour each fart;
Bodily functions play their part.
I take my underpants off to Art.

[23 September 1995]

HUMPHREY THE DOWNING STREET CAT

*Went missing, believed, erroneously, dead. Written with,
and largely by, JT.*

Humphrey lives in Downing Street,
His address is Number Ten.
His office is Westminster;
His alarm clock is Big Ben.

Humphrey saw off Mrs T,
And settled down with Norma.
The temperature around the place
Grew measurably warmer.

Humphrey is an upright cat,
As all his friends remark,
Though once a certain group of ducks
Went missing from the Park.

The PM leaped to his defence;
It didn't come to trial.
"Natural causes," he explained.
They closed the murder file.

Humphrey prowled the corridors
And kept the mice at bay.
The cabinet were all struck dumb
When Humphrey went away.

Yes, suddenly he wasn't there.
The very worst was feared.
His health had not been very good;
Obituaries appeared.

But cats are indestructible,
As everybody knows.
He went away and now he's back.
That's just the way it goes.

Middle England is relieved;
The nation breathes again,
As Humphrey takes his rightful place
Back home at Number Ten.

[7 October 1995]

IF - *(Only I Had Written That One)*

*The nation voted Kipling's 'If-' the most popular poem
for National Poetry Day.*

If you can write a poetry that's manly,
    That gives it to them straight, right on the chin;
That's redolent of Livingstone and Stanley -
    A little stubbly swagger and a grin;
If you can claim of Fate that we can lick it
    Providing everybody plays the game
(And that the game we play, of course, is cricket)
    And strongly hint that things should stay the same:

If you're at home with tweedy E.M.Forster,
    The Empire, Eton collars and full rhymes;
And think each modern poet an imposter
    And free verse up there with the greatest crimes;
If you can fill your work with ringing phrases
    That people quote and get to know by heart
(A rhetorician's trick that still amazes
    The quieter souls who practise this great art):

If you can make the page your little rostrum
    And talk, without quite shouting, pretty loud;
If you can gild each moralistic nostrum
    You'll gain the plaudits of the flattered crowd.
What's more, your fans will hog each hotline minute
    To register unwithering regard.
If there's a competition, why, you'll win it
    And be acclaimed the Nation's Favourite Bard!

[21 October 1995]

ASYLUM

The government's shameful assault on those least capable of standing up for themselves was extended to include asylum seekers. Selected countries with very dubious human rights records were put on a 'white' list, from which bona fide asylum seekers were not expected. Others were to be starved out by being deprived of all social benefits.

Another scrounger. Step this way.
Don't get your hopes up. You won't stay.

Asylum! Pull the other one.
It's obvious you are on the run

From poverty and want a slice
Of our rich cake. It would nice,

As any fool can see - that's why
We have the rules that we apply.

We'll take down your particulars,
But just be warned, you'll find that scars

Are not admissible as proof.
I'm sorry if we seem aloof,

Unkind or callouse even. You
Must see we have a job to do.

Here's something that you may have missed.
Your country's on our little list

Of places that it's safe to be,
And that has shaped our policy.

It may come as a sad surprise
If you've believed in all those lies

Put out by Amnesty and co,
But I assure you it is so.

And given that it is the case,
We cannot offer you a place.

If you would understand a nation
Review its stand on immigration.

Our basic instinct whispers: Black.
Election coming. Send 'em back.

[14 November 1995]

THIS TIME

I'm giving it up altogether;
I will not succumb any more,
And when I am tempted at parties,
I'll answer, No thanks, I am sure.

It'll make me a much better person,
To prove that I can do without.
It'll make my life freer and purer;
Of that I've no shadow of doubt.

It'll prove I've got inner resources;
It'll show that my will-power's immense.
I'll become a bit of a byword
For restraint and sound common sense.

I won't be the least bit self-righteous
In my role as a secular saint.
My forbearance will earn admiration,
My fortitude make others faint.

I've had the odd moment of panic.
Can I really resist and not crack?
But now that I've said that I'll do it,
I'm convinced there'll be no going back.

I know if you look at the record,
I've made such commitments before.
But this time I really am certain,
I won't be doing that any more.

[30 December 1995]

OLD SONG FOR A NEW YEAR

The new year brings new terrors
But we can't adjust our mirrors,
        For what we've left behind is still ahead.
Who's that shifty mister hitching?
Does he know the girl that's missing?
        Does he know the girl that's missing is now dead?

There are blood pools in the potholes,
There are screams from ill-lit stairwells.
        A month of Sundays leads to one arrest.
There's a sense of slow regression
And the overall impression
        Is that somehow we have failed a vital test.

There are mad cows in the meadows,
Naked corpses in the hedgerows -
        A million tyres whine past without a pause.
Everyone's an individual
And self-interest's residual,
        But still we claim to trust in natural laws.

The road rage in the fast lane
Lights an ember in the tired brain
        That bursts into a sudden flame of hate.
We have downsized our compassion
And dressed violence up as fashion.
        A change of heart may prove a little late.

                        [13 January 1996]

SCOTT FREE-FOR-ALL

The Scott report finally came out, full of damning evidence of Ministerial lies and cover-ups. But though the loaded revolver was left on the table in the Officers' Mess, no one was remotely tempted to do the decent thing.

When is a rule-change not a rule-change?
When is a guideline no longer a guide?
When is sophistry not duplicity?
That is a ticklish one to decide.

What is the name for misinformation
Given in public with hand on heart
And then repeated in countless letters?
A game of semantics, a work of art?

How many featly dancing angels
Can pirouette on the head of a pin?
How many dubious moral contortions
Will it take to save a Minister's skin?

Incredible cock-ups, mishaps, happen,
Either by accident or design.
Who though assumes responsibility?
When will anyone ever resign?

Who would you rather have in office,
A competent liar or bungling clown?
I suspect we'd all prefer to have neither
As a serving officer of the Crown.

[24 February 1996]

ROYAL RHYME

*The conflict between Prince Charles and Lady Diana
finally came to a head with the announcement that they
were to divorce.*

It used to be different at court
When wives and husbands fought.
When Henry Tudor decided
He'd had enough of a bride, he'd
Simply make plans to remove her
Like a bit of fluff with a hoover.

So adorable Anne Boleyn
Was accused of a heinous sin -
Of causing a major riot
In the tights of Sir Thomas Wyatt,
And, to put the case mildly,
Of generally acting wildly.

Off to the Tower she was sent,
And Henry didn't relent.
A trumped-up charge was read:
"Off with her head," he said.
Then he hummed "Anything goes
When I'm through with an English rose."

But those were the days of yore;
Things aren't like that any more.
These days hostility rages
In headlines across front pages,
With attacks and then counter attacks
Replacing the old-fashioned axe.

[8 March 1996]

BSE: A MODEST PROPOSAL
(Or how to save our tax-cuts at someone else's expense)

The risk-to-profit ratio was low.
The experts that we paid for told us so.

(The others talked unpatriotic rot
And should have been, with hindsight, quietly shot.)

Still, never mind, we've got another wheeze.
The farmers may be driven to their knees,

But what about defence? The MoD
Could do much worse than run with BSE.

Germ-warfare tried and tested on the nation -
The perfect spin-off from deregulation.

Imagine how the lethal stuff would sell:
CJD – The Additive From Hell!

We'd all take pride in stock-cubed British herds
Flogged off to help Iraq thin out the Kurds.

You question if it really could be done?
We nearly made it with the Super Gun...

[6 April 1996]

ODE ON A GOAL
For Andrew Bolton

*However much public exasperation and private grief
Paul Gascoigne generates, there's no denying his
sublime footballing skills. He had a great European
Cup, and one of his goals against Scotland was truly
that rare phenomenon, poetry in motion.*

How good was Gascoigne's goal?
As good as the tarts the knave stole,
As good as a cream-stuffed profiterole
Wolfed whole.

And how good was his left foot?
Better than the one in his right boot
With which he elected to shoot?
That's moot.

Suffice it to say his first touch
Left little but straws at which to clutch.
Too good for the Scots? - Or the Dutch,
Oh, much.

So talk not the haircut,
The incipient beer-gut
Or of the man's being a fruit-and-nut
Case, but

Savour simply the sublime control
Like angels performing rock'n'roll
On the dance-floor of a pinhead. Extol
That goal!

[29 June 1996]

HINTS FOR HOMEWORKERS

Homeworking has its good points -
Forget about the bus,
And rush-hour crowds and tube strikes
Have no effect on us.

The downside is the effort
It takes to fill a day
When all you've got ahead of you
Is work to earn your pay.

The routine I've developed
Is big on washing up.
Take each item separately,
Wash, rinse and dry each cup.

Another thing I'd mention
That really helps time pass is
Tightening up those little screws
On specs, if you wear glasses.

Some people check their cheque stubs;
Others clean their shoes.
Displacement chores are plentiful;
It's up to you to choose.

You'll find your own distractions,
(And don't forget the phone).
There's nothing like a day to fill
When you are on your own.

[10 August 1996]

THAT SINKING FEELING

My laptop computer's gone down.
It seemed to go just like that.
I've checked it's properly plugged in;
I don't think the battery's flat.

I'm still getting stuff on the screen;
The icons appear as they should.
But they won't respond to the mouse,
So that is no earthly good.

It goes through its termite clicks
But then it does nothing at all.
I've tried it again and again.
It's driving me right up the wall.

You ought to back up as you go.
Oh I know, there's no need to explain.
But I didn't, so now I have lost
Hours of my work down the drain.

Don't panic, Don't panic, you'll say,
But I say Why the hell not?
If I want to panic, I'll panic,
And I want to panic a lot.

Would a call to Samaritans help?
It's filling my soul with despair.
And the worst thing about it of all
Is - I can't even play Solitaire!

[2 November 1996]

POLL UP! POLL UP!

Election fever's here once more.
The knives are out, it's open war,
      With thrust and counter-thrust.
They'll soon be knocking on the door
With all the stuff we've heard before:
      We're the ones to trust!

The country's in a parlous state;
The Tory party's left it late;
      Their chances must be slim.
But Major will not hesitate
To bluster that the country's fate
      Is only safe with him.

His party's split from top to toe;
Some say 'Euro'; some say 'No!';
      They're hardly closing ranks.
In fact we've never seen a show
So steeped in internicine woe:
      For which, Oh Lord, much thanks.

But all the same, they still think they
Should be entrusted with the way
      Ahead for five more years.
They'll bellow that the future's grey;
A Labour government, they'll bray,
      Can only end in tears.

Despite their record, it's amazing,
They've tougher skin than double-glazing
      Salesmen on the prowl.
Out they come with all guns blazing -
Raucous, rancorous, anthem-raising
      Cheek by gleaming jowl.

The Tory press is out for Blair -
Those demon eyes, that thinning hair:
      No Mr Nice Guy now.
When chips are down they hardly care
If what they say is true or fair:
      Just set him up, then Pow!

And Paddy Ashdown gets it too,
With all his wishy-washy crew
      Of Liberal-Democrats;
They haven't got a chance, it's true,
But still it's time to turn the screw
      And write them off as prats.

We've fallen for it in the past;
Perhaps they think it's bound to last.
      Poll up, poll up! they cry.
Think before your vote is cast;
Everything's improving fast!
      One final Tory lie.

They've done the country endless harm
And yet with their obnoxious charm
      They want to patronise
Electors with a wide-flung arm
Or bribe them with a well-greased palm
      - Tax cuts, surprise, surprise!

You have to marvel at the gall
With which they're striving to forestall
      The loss of each last seat;
But they are up against the wall
And one last shove will send them all
      Howling to defeat.

[30 November 1996]